To my wonderful daughter Shaliah, and all children with challenges. Let your light shine and your voice be heard. You can make it! We love you!

Ordering Information:
For details, contact- sheldon@sydspinkbookshelf.com
Paperback ISBN: 979-8-218-30814-8
EBook ISBN: 979-8-218-30815-5

Leah's Voice

Written By: Sheldon D. Harrison
Illustrated by: Travis A. Thompson

Hello. My name is Leah! I am happy to meet you! I look forward to sharing with you about how I use my voice! I was born with cerebral palsy, so my arms, legs, and hands don't quite work the same way as most children. This is my purple wheelchair! My family and others help me by using it to take me to the places that I need to go. Even though I don't have many words, I still use my **voice**! And so can you! Come on! Let me show you! Follow me!

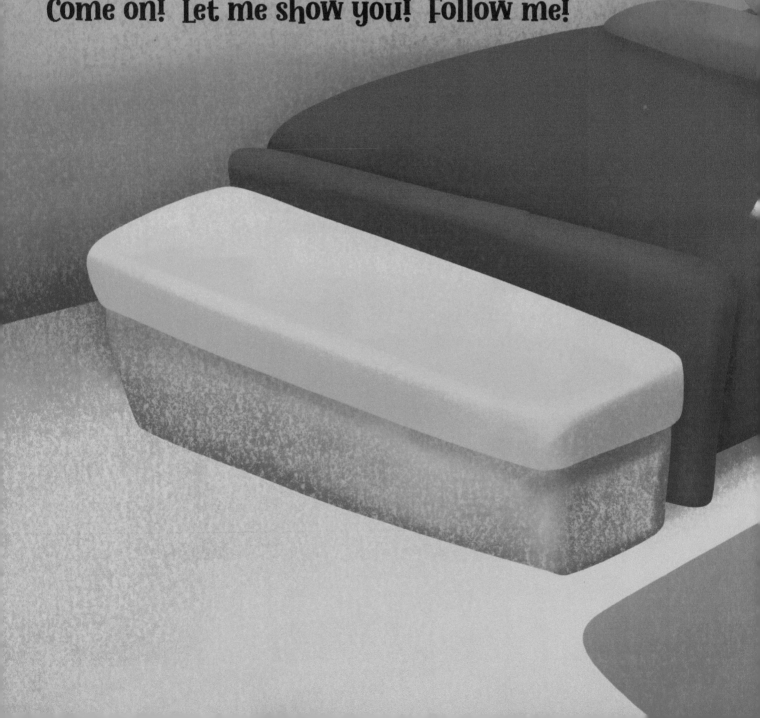

I like going to school. My classmates are my friends and they are all different just like me. Even though each one of our VOICES are different, We all have fun together. We have one another and We're just like family. One of my favorite parts of the day is when my teacher takes me for a trip outside to our play area or down the school hallway.

What's your favorite place to use your VOICE at school?!

My parents and I have to go see the doctor for my checkups. There are always so many toys there that I love to play with! The doctor will normally ask my parents a lot of questions to make sure that I'm ok. And even though I am living with my disability, I am better than I used to be! I use my **voice** to tell the doctor that since I am happy, that means that I'm ok! Sometimes I have to stay there over night, to finish all of my testing, but my family is there with me and we have fun!

I really like When my family takes me out to eat at my favorite restaurant! We don't go very often, so it's always a treat for me! I have a BIG appetite! YUMMY! When it's time to take my order, I use my **voice** to tell the server what I want. Being there is so exciting for me, that sometimes my voice get's really LOUD! And when my voice get's really loud, some other people in the restaurant get uncomfortable and begin to complain.

That's when my daddy takes me outside and plays with me! He likes me to use my VOICE as much as I want! We still have a great time!

Do you like to use your VOICE at your favorite restaurant?

Going to church with my family is the BEST! Everyone is happy there, and we all get to use our **VOICE** the entire time!! Mommy sings all of the songs! My sister sits next to me and claps her hands! Daddy is the pastor! Sometimes church is so fun and I get so happy that I do a little dance in my chair!!

What does your happy dance look like?

Do you like to use your **VOICE** at your favorite place to visit on the weekends?

Listening to music and singing songs is what I use my voice for all the time! I am always singing in the car when we go places! Sometimes my sister joins me, and we put on a concert! She uses her voice at the same time that I use mine and we have such a good time, making music together! My sister plays with me all the time!

What is your favorite song?
Do you like to use your voice to sing songs?!

When we go to the grocery store, there are always so many things and people to see!! There is always someone on every isle that I can't help using my VOICE to greet them with a hello! I see other kids there as well sometimes, and I speak to them as well! It's always good to see some of my classmates in the store! Mommy likes to push me around until we eventually have to go!

Do you like to use your VOICE in the grocery store?!

When I am ready to eat I crawl to my special dinner table. Once I make it there, I use my VOICE to tell my parents that I'm READY TO EAT! Then they make me something tasty to eat and bring it to the table. My parents are good cooks. And it's like they always know exactly what I want to eat!

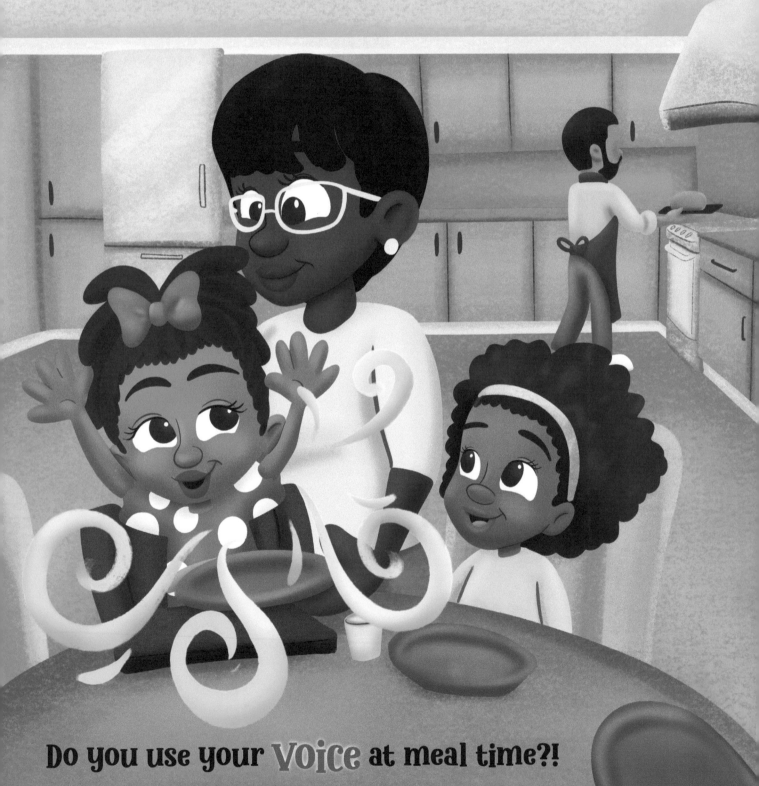

Do you use your VOICE at meal time?!

I'm not always tired enough to fall asleep at bedtime, so I use my VOICE to let my parents know that I want to stay up and play. But they still carry me to my room and lay me down in my bed, because we have an early morning. Daddy holds my hand after putting me to bed, and then he closes his eyes and begins to talk to someone about me, but there is no one else in my room except us.

There are times when I see tears fall from his eyes as he is talking to the invisible person. I always tell him that I am OK, and that he doesn't have to cry. Then he gives me the BIGGEST hug, tells me that he loves me, and he tells me goodnight!

Do you use your VOICE at bed time?!

Don't let anything or anyone discourage
who you are meant to be!

There is no limit to where you can go!

There is no limit to what you can do!

SAY what you can do and DO IT!

SAY who you are and BE IT!

SAY where you are going and GO THERE!

Take it from me, it doesn't matter what you
DON'T have, just use what you DO have! Use your
VOICE to thank those who help you, and listen
to those who LOVE YOU!!

Your VOICE is your SUPER POWER, and you
DESERVE to be HEARD!

Sheldon D. Harrison

I am the author of books such as Leah's Voice, who loves to write stories that inspire both children and adults. I enjoy time with family!